One Year | Year One

Apple E S

BookLeaf Publishing

Presentation by *BookLeaf Publishing*

Web: www.bookleafpub.com

E-mail: info@bookleafpub.com

ISBN: 9789357215763

First edition 2023

Mom, dad, and Tita Jane, this book is for you, thank you for the lessons and foundations, and for the life that I have. Mom and dad, I miss you both very much. Tita, I will see you soon.

ACKNOWLEDGEMENT

To my pillars, Mich, Sally, PJ, Raffy and Junice - thank you so much for giving me your honesty, love, kindness and support. To Harry, thank you for the extra eye - and for everything extra. To Ma Sol, Camille and Alyssa, thank you.

PREFACE

A compilation of poems that have been inspired by all of the events spanning over just one year. A true-to-life example of the ups and downs of the wheel of life. This book will take you through a journey of a series of events, from living a perfect life to almost losing life itself - spanning just over 12 months. Ultimately culminating in a sublime, yet moving process of self-love, self-discovery and repossessing self-worth.

Prelude

A series of feelings expressed,
From being happy to be depressed,
Episodes of unfortunate events,
Empowering lyrics of contents,
Expressed through words written on paper,
Poems that are all truly from the heart's shaper.

Twelve months of anguish,
Twelve months of pain.
Twelve months of happiness,
A mixture of losses and gains.

A snippet of a life lived,
A snapshot of a story untold.
An extract of actions committed,
A year's worth of karma admitted.

Experiences garnered over one year,
A blend of laughter and some with tears.
Now this life's chapter coming to an end,
Year One is about to start; ready, set, MEND!

The Fast Lane

Waking up to the smell of some cooked
perfection,
Every detail of the day is with attention.
Luxurious brunches then shopping in the
mornings,
While soirées and merry making filled one's
evenings.

Traveling to a foreign land on the weekends,
Sunny beaches or explore a city with friends.
On a yacht, sailing through the Caribbeans,
Or jet-setting somewhere in the Aegean.

Perhaps breakfast in New York for the day,
Then Michelin star dinner all the way.
Black ties and Masquerade balls true cliche,
Private events with unlimited buffet.

Thinking that time was never of the essence,
Fuelled by youth, one's truly quintessence.
Non-consequential life is truly a bliss,
Always chasing for Dionysian's kiss.

Truly, one can say that life was perfect,
Being in the fast lane, life was well-kept.
The rush can make one feel invincible,
Powered by money, truly formidable.

The Young'un

Half-past eleven in the evening,
Midsummer night's dreaming.
A bar full of people merry making,
A handsome, tall man came in wondering.

With one look from those green eyes,
The noise, the world around us dies.
With one word, one smile from those lips,
Train of thoughts, little by little slips.

An hour turned into a year,
Mixture of laughter and tears.
The best man in the kitchen I know,
Dishes just like in a cooking show

At a young age of twenty-six,
You possessed the ability to fix.
Thank you for the support you gave,
When my mother entered her grave.

Blue

Half past six and one was late,
She did not anticipate.
Bustling busy city lives,
Mixing with so many types.

In a mundane blue lace dress,
She hopes he will be impressed.
To her surprise, he then smiles,
In a blue suit without a tie.

He is a lawyer, deprived of life,
While live to the fullest, she thrives.
With Happiness, they shared the night,
Time flew by like the speed of light.

And the time came that they must go,
But he was not ready, he said, “no”.
“Spend the night”, he pleads to her,
She was spellbound, by the time they shared.

The night was magical, least expected,
They shared together, time consecrated.
The blue lace dress was on his bedroom floor,
But his smile has opened up her heart’s door.

Tropic of Cancer

One day I woke up,
being eaten from within,
Silence, time’s ticking.

Ibiza

Sixteenth of July, it was a sunny Friday,
The excitement is overflowing I should say.
As the warm breeze hits my face,
Sol is greeting me with his daze.
The salty air envelops my lungs,
As I started speaking in tongues.

As the clock strikes one,
All of my hesitations are gone.
I see you walking out of the door,
I can feel the happiness from my core.
I hid in silence for a surprise,
But I can't put my excitement in disguise.

I said, 'hello' with a can of beer,
To your utter delight, you hugged me near.
The smell of Chanel on your skin
As you kiss me, pulling me tightly in.
Your strong arms wrapped around me,
There is truly no other place I'd rather be.

For dinner, we stared at the setting Sun,
For deserts, promenaded holding hands.
As the sea breeze caresses my hair,
You hold me close, full of care.

Like a fragile little China doll,
Like a piece of glass that cannot fall.

As the stars, as our only witness,
Your gaze digs deeper into my wellness.
Your voice gives a sense of contentment,
Like a Lukewarm bath of enticement.

In four days, my heart you captured,
Inhibitions gone; walls are all shattered.
In four nights, my body and soul you earned,
It truly feels like the tables have been turned.

I am so grateful for the time you gave,
For your body, mind and soul, I crave.
Ibiza will never be the same again,
I hope we will be back there, together again.

Fe + Au

She was named after iron,
Strong and sturdy like the belt of Orion.
But also soft, beautiful and malleable,
Generous, giving but infallible.

She has the ability to command,
Even the Spanish Armada by hand.
Sacrificing her body and soul,
For her family she gives her all.

As a healer she gives care,
To strangers who are cold and bare.
She provides love, life of passion she shares
To the unfamiliar, she breathes life and air.

Dubbed the lady of Iron,
She came from a family of dragons.
With a sharp tongue and a deadly mouth,
She breathes fire at enemies with just one shout.
But her true nature lies within,
Kind, generous, loving a sure win.

He was named after gold,
Very precious, rare and bold.
Built like Maui, tall and wide,
But with gentleness and love as his guide.

He wields his sword of lead to draw,
As a master builder, designs without a flaw.
As he conquered the unforgiving land of Black
Gold,
With his square and compass, he portrayed
stories untold.

He had the opportunity of a lifetime,
To garner endless amounts of dime.
But he chose to be a servant,
To his only princess with zeal most fervent.
He chose a life of servitude and carriage,
To his queen and spoiled child without
disparage.

As the only child of Iron and Gold,
Now it's my turn to prove that I am bold.
To demonstrate that I am worthy,
Of all the sacrifices and the life, they gave me.

Now that the iron has rusted and the gold faded,
I am left alone as I navigate this world jaded.
There's a hollow chasm within the daughter,
Missing pieces of a mother and a father.

I am lost and lonely, alone in this world,
A true version of an orphan, truly unfurled.

“Fe’au” in Samoan is a dear word,
“To wait for somebody” is heard.
I will wait and wait for that blessed day,
When both of you are with me to stay.

Ohana

As the month of December comes
Accompanied by grief's cold hums.
Announced by melancholy's drums,
Head pointed to unnerving guns.

It is cold and dreary,
Makes one very weary.
With nowhere else to go,
No family, friends or foe.

An invitation sent from above,
Received from a white kindred dove.
His family is more than happy,
To have the orphan, nothing too fancy.

The orphan was truly humbled,
"Nuisance, am I not?", she mumbled.
He answered that it was more than well,
He wants to save her from her own hell.

'Ohana' in Hawaiian means family,
Nobody gets left behind, naturally.
Welcomed with open hearts and arms,
The orphan was now safe from harm.

The orphan shows a grateful behavior,
For the Tiller's warm welcome, her savior.
Now her December is finally warm,
Even if she's still trapped in grief's arms.
As now she has new people to stay,
In her heart they will be her family, per say.

Silver Lining

Days and weeks have gone by,
Without incidents I don't know why.
A false sense of safety was ensured,
That everything was fine, rest assured.

Except for the all-consuming grief,
It was made very clear and quite brief.
Not to mention the Cancer that devour,
The body from within, every hour.

Happiness once again, was in sight,
That it was alright to take a flight.
Runaway from the problems at present,
Since it's Christmas, t'was indeed a present.
That a couple of days won't matter,
Thirsty for strength, like it was water.

Being thankful for a lovely man,
For everything that he can.
Being thankful for a life of survival,
Waiting for true happiness' arrival.

So, a light of kindness was given,
For the souls as a beacon back to heaven.
A light of love for the mother and father a miss,
Hoping to have that one very last kiss.

Fire

The light you left behind,
For the souls to follow home.
The light that was kind,
Now is like the fires of Rome.

The light you left behind,
Destroyed everything in its path.
The light that was kind,
Now you taste its wrath.

Motherless and fatherless,
Now you are homeless.
Penniless with sickness,
This fire has left you lifeless.

The Gospel of Luke

He came in the middle of the crucifixions,
When people are throwing their rocks of
accusations.
Piercing her heart like the spear of Longinus,
She's crying for help to the goddess Venus.

Like in Luke chapter eight verse two,
Seven demons within me, too.
Like Mary Magdalene cries for mercy,
Assaulted by life's unending fury.
But like Jesus, he came and saved me,
From tormented life, I thank thee eternally.

When afflicted by countless maladies,
He was there to help with the commodities.
In Luke chapter five verse thirteen,
You have healed me from within.

Luke chapter twelve verse fifty-nine,
Now I must pay my long overdue fines.
Life mixed with grief and sadness,
Toxicity and insecurities at its finest.

Luke chapter twenty-two verse five,
I have sold you out while you cried.

Cause' the pain that I delivered to you,
Hurting more than a crown of thrones pierced through.

Luke chapter six verse twenty-one,
The ultimate damage has been done.
"Happy are those who weep now",
I'll let you go, that's my vow.

Luke chapter seven verse forty-seven,
Many are my sins, to be in heaven.
But I ask for forgiveness as I only love much,
Desire for Judas' kiss and heavenly touch.

"Eli, Eli, Lama Sabachthani", Father, why have you truly forsaken me?
All I ever wanted was to love him thoroughly.
But the anguish of yesterday still lingers,
I must let him go, happiness slipping through his fingers.

My last confession was outdated,
Even hundreds of 'Hail Marys' won't make it.
Only a lifelong penance from within,
So, forgive me father for I have sinned.

"Untitled"

Melancholy's here
Helpless, alone and in fear
Death calling me near.

Empath

Both gift and a curse of trait,
Empathy is truly great.
The ability to share,
Feelings of others to bear.

She is a strong Nubian goddess,
That shows her emotional prowess.
To everybody she loves dear,
Her greatest power, a listening ear.

Her emotional storage is vast,
Like a net in the ocean's cast.
Her care for others is all self-consuming,
She puts people first, self-sacrificing.

She was one of the pillars that held,
The sane's insanity is truly compelled.
She kept the north tower of love,
Like she came down from up above.

Her love is so pure that it's rare,
So precious and crucial like air.
And when death was calling in one's ear,
She shared her love and her tears.

Lucky is an understatement, least to say.
One cannot express gratitude till the last day.
Thank you for everything I can convey,
I love you truly, with all of my heart every day.

Light Bender

Logic and eloquence are his power,
Like a beacon of light on the tower.
The ability to turn bad situations up,
With a mature method of a grownup.

Six years of friendship is not long,
But one would say the bond is very strong.
Always a helping hand in times of need,
A prime adviser and a guidance to heed.

Judgment has never been given,
To any of the wrong doings written.
Out of the few, a genuine friend,
Always the one to reach out in the end.

Thank you for everything and for the light,
And for your strength and your might.
Thank you for the happiness you channel,
Especially the light at the end of the tunnel.

A healer by profession,
A friend by selection.
A family by ascension,
A keeper by devotion.

Four-Foot Eleven-Inches

Truly big things come from small package,
From a four-foot eleven-inch savage.
With a lovely, positive mindset to boot,
She never misses when she shoots.

Seven years of friendship evolved,
From a toxic person involved.
Sharing the same ideology,
That positivity is the new supremacy.

Refuses to give up on life and love,
She always reaches the stars above.
Even though that she's quite short,
God is behind her, here henceforth.

Plenty of days and nights are shared,
Laughter and tears sometimes paired.
Plenty of relationship have been done,
But she was always there, never gone.

Thank you for the love and given ears,
And for all the dried-up tears.
Gratitude is from the heart and soul,
I will always catch you if you ever fall.

The Unsung Hero

You have been there for five-year straight,
I sometimes forget what's the date.
Our first meeting was coincidental,
Serendipitous, magical and accidental.

You have helped me financially,
When my mother died so suddenly.
You gave me strength when I was weak,
When my father went, so to speak.

You always show up when I am down,
Saving me from death, so I won't drown.
You take me away when things are bleak,
So, clarity can come when I seek.

I am sorry for the shortcomings in my life
And when everything feels like a sharp knife.
I am sorry that I cannot give more to you,
I can only show gratitude that I can do.

I cannot thank you enough my friend,
But I can promise we are till the end.
You are a family to me no matter what,
You are the unsung hero in my heart.

Magnesium

Like a crucial element to the planet,
You are essential to my health.
Like an important electrolyte,
You give me my sense of sight.

Like a metal, you are hard and stern,
Ready to teach a lesson to learn.
But like a beautiful spring afternoon,
So cool and tepid like a lagoon.

You have been there since I was born,
Giving me love, guidance, never forlorn.
You have sacrificed your life for me,
And I can never ever thank thee.

I promise to take care of you,
And love you endlessly too.
I will try my best to cherish,
Mom and dad's wishes will never perish.

Now that the Iron and the Gold are depleted,
Double dose of Magnesium is really needed.
Thank you so much for everything,
Without you I will be nothing.

I love you endlessly,
Unconditionally.

Valescere

Experiences are the greatest teachers,
While time and space are the best healers.
Strength is regained from the mixture of the two,
But perseverance is very crucial too.

One must allow experience to teach,
What lessons and expectations to reach.
In recovery, perseverance is a must,
So, one can have the strength to stand up and
wipe off the dust.

Bravery is also quite essential,
To face the truth and cut denial.
As Time can take quite a while,
Like slowly sailing down the Nile.
So having patience is necessary,
To know how to tackle your many adversaries,

Lastly, love is very much needed,
Self-love must be present conceded,
For one to recover from the pain,
And remove what's left of the stain.

To begin to grow strong again,
Always believe in yourself now and then,

Now take this knowledge as you may,
So that you have what you need to face the day.

Metamorphosis

All my life I have waited,
For a god's miracle, predated.
For when what's inside comes out,
And be free from the screams and the shouts.

I have always felt like a stranger,
Even to myself and to my own skin.
Feeling claustrophobic and endangered,
Like somebody from the outside looking in.

Like trekking an unknown jungle,
Left nothing for any defense.
Lost in a labyrinthine maze,
Confused, broken with dulled senses.

But the Bellringer rang the bell,
That signaled the end of being in hell.
As I close my eyes into the cold darkness,
The promise of happiness in starkness.

I open my eyes to a whole new world,
Alas, my cries of desperations are heard.
The outside is now at peace with what's within.
A new and wonderful life can now begin.

Sunrise

Morning has broken
One heart two hands are open
For God has spoken.

Gratitude

God, I thank thee, for
Righteous eyes to see, the
Ample love from people,
Truly it has been my staple.
I want to thank my family,
Thank you for loving me,
Unconditionally.
Dear reader, to you as well,
Endless gratitude I spell.

www.ingramcontent.com/pod-product-compliance
Lightning Source LLC
Chambersburg PA
CBHW051748130826
49812CB00033B/1058

* 9 7 8 9 3 5 7 2 1 5 7 6 3 *